EX LIBRIS

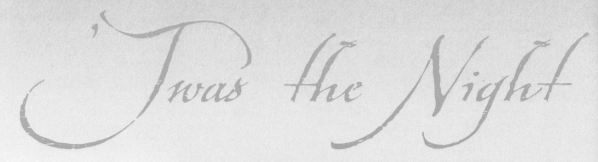

'Twas the Night

OR
ACCOUNT OF
A VISIT FROM
ST. NICHOLAS

❧❧❧❧❧❧❧❧❧

ANONYMOUS

❧

ILLUSTRATED BY
MATT TAVARES

WALKER BOOKS
AND SUBSIDIARIES

LONDON · BOSTON · SYDNEY · AUCKLAND

Before Christmas

To Sarah, my wife

The illustrator would like to thank Art Usher; Tobin Anderson; The
Museum of Fine Arts, Boston; The Nichols House Museum; The Gibson
House Museum; Kennebec Morgan Horse Farm; Manuel, Jane, Melissa,
and Sarah P. Tavares; Lauren and Rob Fogarty; Shannon, Ryan,
Lu–Ann, and Bob Hickey; Pauline Hickey; Andrew Grasso; the Swanton
family; Rosemary Stimola; Chris Paul; and Kara LaReau.

First published 2002 by Walker Books Ltd
87 Vauxhall Walk, London SE11 5HJ

This edition published 2006

2 4 6 8 10 9 7 5 3 1

Illustrations © 2002 Matt Tavares

This book has been typeset in Dickens

Printed in Italy

British Library Cataloguing in Publication Data:
a catalogue record for this book is available
from the British Library

ISBN–13: 978–1–4063–0227–1
ISBN–10: 1–4063–0227–9

www.walkerbooks.co.uk

A Note from the Illustrator

In December of 1823, a newspaper in upstate New York called the TROY SENTINEL printed an anonymous poem entitled "Account of a Visit from St. Nicholas." This was the first time many children in America had ever heard of St. Nicholas. Naturally, they wondered what might happen if they hung their stockings by the chimney, just like the children in the poem. On Christmas Eve of that year, many tried it.

Sure enough, when those children awoke on Christmas morning, they were greeted by the sweet smells of sugarplums and the thrill of new, hand-carved toys. News of this incredible phenomenon spread quickly throughout the world, and St. Nicholas — or Santa Claus, as he is now known — has been a very busy man ever since.

In 1844, a man named Clement C. Moore claimed authorship of "Account of a Visit from St. Nicholas." Since then, many scholars have contested that claim and have even named other possible authors, so we may never know the identity of the anonymous writer. Over the years, the poem has also undergone changes. It has become known to many by a different title, 'TWAS THE NIGHT BEFORE CHRISTMAS, after its opening line. Also, many editors have taken liberties in altering its original punctuation and spelling. Some have even changed the names of Santa's reindeer. But the words in the edition you're about to read appear exactly as they did when "Account of a Visit from St. Nicholas" was first published anonymously in the TROY SENTINEL on December 23, 1823.

Happy Christmas!
Matt Tavares

'Twas the night before Christmas,

when all thro' the house,

Not a creature was stirring,

not even a mouse;

The stockings were hung

by the chimney with care,

In hopes that St. Nicholas

soon would be there;

The children were nestled
all snug in their beds,
While visions of sugar plums
danc'd in their heads,
And Mama in her 'kerchief,
and I in my cap,
Had just settled our brains
for a long winter's nap —

When out on the lawn
    there arose such a clatter,
I sprang from the bed
    to see what was the matter.
Away to the window
    I flew like a flash,
Tore open the shutters,
    and threw up the sash.

The moon on the breast of the new fallen snow,

Gave the lustre of mid-day to objects below;

When, what to my wondering eyes should appear,

But a miniature sleigh, and eight tiny rein-deer,

With a little old driver, so lively and quick,

I knew in a moment it must be St. Nick.

More rapid than eagles his coursers they came,
And he whistled, and shouted, and call'd them by name:
"Now! Dasher, now! Dancer, now! Prancer, and Vixen,

"On! Comet, on! Cupid, on! Dunder and Blixem;

"To the top of the porch! to the top of the wall!

"Now dash away! dash away! dash away all!"

As dry leaves before the wild hurricane fly,
When they meet with an obstacle, mount to the sky;

So up to the house-top the coursers they flew,
With the sleigh full of Toys — and St. Nicholas too:

And then in a twinkling,
 I heard on the roof
The prancing and pawing
 of each little hoof.
As I drew in my head,
 and was turning around,
Down the chimney St. Nicholas
 came with a bound:

He was dress'd all in fur,
    from his head to his foot,
And his clothes were all tarnish'd
    with ashes and soot;
A bundle of toys was
    flung on his back,
And he look'd like a peddler
    just opening his pack:

His eyes — how they twinkled!
his dimples how merry,
His cheeks were like roses,
his nose like a cherry;
His droll little mouth was
drawn up like a bow.
And the beard of his chin
was as white as the snow;
The stump of a pipe
he held tight in his teeth,
And the smoke it encircled
his head like a wreath.

He had a broad face, and a
    little round belly
That shook when he laugh'd,
    like a bowl full of jelly:
He was chubby and plump,
    a right jolly old elf,
And I laugh'd when I saw him
    in spite of myself;
A wink of his eye and a twist
    of his head
Soon gave me to know I had
    nothing to dread.

He spoke not a word, but
    went straight to his work,
And fill'd all the stockings;
    then turn'd with a jerk,
And laying his finger
    aside of his nose
And giving a nod,
    up the chimney he rose.

He sprung to his sleigh, to his team gave a whistle,
And away they all flew, like the down of a thistle:

But I heard him exclaim,

       ere he drove out of sight —

Happy Christmas to all,

and to all a good night.